Fantastic Kids
Young Artists

David Paris

112005

Consultants

Roy Herweck
Muralist

Publishing Credits

Rachelle Cracchiolo, M.S.Ed., *Publisher*
Conni Medina, M.A.Ed., *Managing Editor*
Nika Fabienke, Ed.D., *Series Developer*
June Kikuchi, *Content Director*
John Leach, *Assistant Editor*
Kevin Pham, *Graphic Designer*

TIME For Kids and the TIME For Kids logo are registered trademarks of TIME Inc. Used under license.

Image Credits: p.4 Pavel Filatov/Alamy Stock Photo; pp.6–7, 7 (from) Chance Yeh/Getty Images; p.8 Musee Marmottan Monet, Paris, France/Bridgeman Images; p.9 Albanpix Ltd/REX/Shutterstock; p.10 (left) Scala/Art Resource, NY; p.11 Harry Ransom Center, University of Texas at Austin, Austin, USA/ © Leemage/Bridgeman Images; pp.12–13 Phil Donaghue/Newscom; pp.14–15 (foreground) Jeffrey R. Staab via Getty Images; p.16 (inset) United Archives GmbH / Alamy Stock Photo; pp.16–17 Richard Levine/Alamy Stock Photo; p.19 (left) Al Levine/NBC/NBCU Photo Bank/Getty Images, (right) Jason Kempin/ Getty Images for the DAILY FRONT ROW; p.20 Emiley Schweich/Everett Collection; pp.20–21 David Bukach/Disney XD via Getty Images; p.22 Stanley Weston/Getty Images; p.23 Anne Frank Fonds - Basel via Getty Images; p.24 McClatchy-Tribune Information Services; p.25 (left) Entertainment Pictures/ Alamy Stock Photo, (right) razorpix/Alamy Stock Photo; all other images from iStock and/or Shutterstock.

Library of Congress Cataloging-in-Publication Data

Names: Paris, David, author.
Title: Fantastic kids : young artists / David Paris.
Description: Huntington Beach, CA : Teacher Created Materials, 2017. | Includes index. | Audience: Grades 4 to 6. | Description based on print version record and CIP data provided by publisher; resource not viewed.
Identifiers: LCCN 2017017374 (print) | LCCN 2017018252 (ebook) | ISBN 9781425853563 (eBook) | ISBN 9781425849825 (pbk.)
Subjects: LCSH: Arts--Juvenile literature. | Child artists--Juvenile literature.
Classification: LCC NX633 (ebook) | LCC NX633 .P37 2017 (print) | DDC 700--dc23
LC record available at https://lccn.loc.gov/2017017374

Teacher Created Materials
5301 Oceanus Drive
Huntington Beach, CA 92649-1030
http://www.tcmpub.com

ISBN 978-1-4258-4982-5

© 2018 Teacher Created Materials, Inc.
Made in China
Nordica.072017.CA21700822

Table of Contents

The Heart of an Artist

Many people **express** themselves through art. Artists share feelings and showcase the beauty around us. Whether it is through paint, song, dance, theater, or words, artists **interpret** the world.

Kids and Art

You may think that only adults can be great artists. But this is not true. Many children are talented artists, too. All people have the ability to create art. They just need to find a way to express their artistic sides. Many famous artists began their **craft** at a young age and went on to have a long career in art.

Writing on the Wall

What are the oldest works of art? Probably cave drawings found in Asia and Europe. They have been dated as far back as 40,000 years ago.

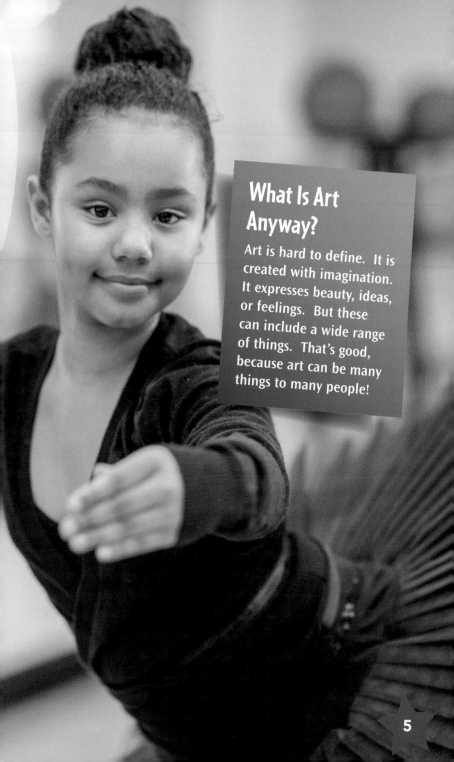

What Is Art Anyway?

Art is hard to define. It is created with imagination. It expresses beauty, ideas, or feelings. But these can include a wide range of things. That's good, because art can be many things to many people!

Brush Up

Painting is a great way for kids to express themselves! There are many young artists whose work is enjoyed by people of all ages.

Abstract Aelita

Aelita Andre (ey-LEE-tuh AHN-drey) is a young **abstract** artist from Australia. When she was two years old, her paintings were in an art show. People who saw her paintings did not realize she was so young. They were very impressed by her art. By the time she was four, her paintings often sold for as much as $10,000 each.

Aelita likes to add objects to her paintings. She has added feathers, plastic figures, or masks to some of her artwork. She has even added glitter.

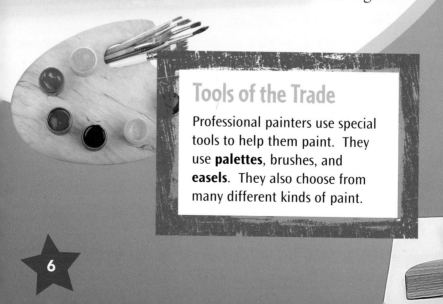

Tools of the Trade

Professional painters use special tools to help them paint. They use **palettes**, brushes, and **easels**. They also choose from many different kinds of paint.

STOP! THINK...

> Why might someone want to become a painter?

> What makes Aelita's artwork unique?

> What types of tools do painters use?

Aelita Andre

Kieron, a Mini Monet

Kieron (KEER-uhn) Williamson is from England. Like many children, Kieron loved coloring and drawing pictures of dinosaurs. His earliest drawings were simple. But he enjoyed art so much that he learned more about it and improved. He started painting using **watercolors**.

By the time he was seven years old, Kieron's paintings were selling for thousands of dollars. His art shows sold out in less than half an hour. No one cared how old he was. Kieron says he is just happy to be able to do what he likes to do—make art.

The Real Monet

Claude Monet was a French painter. His style of painting is called *impressionism*. This art style captures a feeling rather than showing realistic scenes. Monet made over 200 paintings of water lilies.

Walking into a Painting

One of Monet's largest works is in the Museum of Modern Art in New York City. It is 6.5 feet (1.98 meters) tall and almost 42 feet (12.8 meters) long. Standing in front of it can create the feeling of being in a garden.

Kieron Williamson

Growing with Art

Pablo Picasso is one of the world's most famous artists. He had a unique painting style called **cubism**. He also made sculptures and wrote poems and plays. He was very talented.

Picasso started creating art at a young age. When he was seven years old, he studied how to paint and draw with his father, who was also a painter. It is said that when Picasso was 13, his father thought that his son was the better of the two.

> "Every child is an artist. The problem is how to remain an artist once he grows up."

Pablo Picasso

No Stopping Frida

Mexican artist Frida Kahlo was struck by **polio** when she was young. This disease made her childhood very hard. Even so, she became a famous painter.

Song and Dance

Singing is a great way to express yourself. The human voice is a natural instrument. It can make all sorts of sounds. *Pitch* describes how high or low a sound is. The differences between singers' highest pitches and lowest pitches are called *vocal ranges*.

Make Yourself Heard

Jackie Evancho (uh-VENG-koh) is an **opera** singer. She won second place on the TV show *America's Got Talent* in 2010. She was 10 years old at the time. She has released several albums since then. One sold more than one million copies! This is called *going platinum*. Jackie was the youngest **solo** artist to do this in the United States.

Say Goodbye to Stage Fright

Some people get nervous about performing in front of others. This is called *stage fright* and is quite common. It often goes away the more you practice performing. Even simple things such as telling jokes to your friends will help reduce the effects of stage fright.

Jackie Evancho

Changing Voices

As kids grow, their voices often change. This can affect the way that they sing. For boys, the voice change can make it difficult to sing the high notes that they used to be able to reach. Singers must relearn how to sing with their new voices.

Graceful Ballerina

Dancing is another great way to express yourself. There are many types of dance. Each has its own style of movement and music. People can choose one style or mix styles to create their own.

Misty Copeland

❯ What makes an artist?

❯ What are some different forms of art?

❯ Where do artists get their ideas?

Misty Copeland took her first ballet class when she was 13 years old. Most ballet students start at a much younger age. But Misty was **dedicated** and worked hard. She won awards. She joined the American Ballet Theatre five years later. This is a well-known ballet group. She later became a lead dancer in the group. She is the first African American woman to have that position.

Some Kids Do It All

Many children sing and dance. Some also act and play musical instruments. Many talented kids perform in Broadway shows. Broadway is a street in New York City. Many theaters are on or near this street. These theaters show plays and musicals almost every night. The musicals *Annie*, *School of Rock*, and *Matilda* all have kids in their casts.

Many famous adult actors starred in Broadway shows as children. Anna Kendrick is known for the *Pitch Perfect* movies. She was in a show called *High Society* when she was 12. Lea Michele from *Glee* was only nine when she was in the musical *Les Misérables*.

A Performer at Heart

Judy Garland started singing and dancing when she was seven. She later performed in movies and on the radio. You may know her as Dorothy in *The Wizard of Oz*.

billboard for *Annie*

Thrills and Spills

When something goes wrong during a live performance, actors have to think fast. Actors might trip or forget a line. Do they stop the play? No! Actors improvise—they make up lines to move the story along.

Acting Up!

Many kids may think that acting is not for them, but most of them have been acting since they were little. When you were younger, did you play games where you pretended to be a sports star, a singer, an astronaut, a doctor, or a teacher? That was acting!

Some kids really enjoy this type of playacting. The next step for them might be to perform on stage.

Acting in Your Community

Many towns have something called a community theater. This is a place where local people get together to put on plays. There is probably one near you.

There Are No Small Parts

Drew Barrymore is a well-known actress. She got her start very early in the movie *E.T. the Extra-Terrestrial*. She was six years old when she played the role of Gertie. She only had a supporting role but was so talented that people took notice!

Being a Kid

Being in a play or musical can take a lot of time. Professional child actors have to make sure to keep up with their schoolwork. They must make an extra effort to find time to do other things, such as play with their friends.

Battling Monsters

Nathaniel Potvin (PAHT-vihn) started acting when he was 12. He is on a Disney XD series called *Mech-X4*. Before this, he acted in a number of other TV shows.

In *Mech-X4*, Nathaniel plays a character who has special powers. He can control a giant robot with his mind. He works with other kid actors on the show. During filming, he often has to pretend to battle monsters. After filming is done, monsters are digitally added into the scenes. He has to move and react as if the monsters are really there. He even has to talk to pretend people. Acting in this way takes a lot of skill.

"Danger, Will Robinson!"

Bill Mumy started acting on TV in 1961 at the age of six. By 11, he had landed his most famous role as Will Robinson in the adventure show *Lost in Space*. He even had his own (pretend) robot!

Will's robot

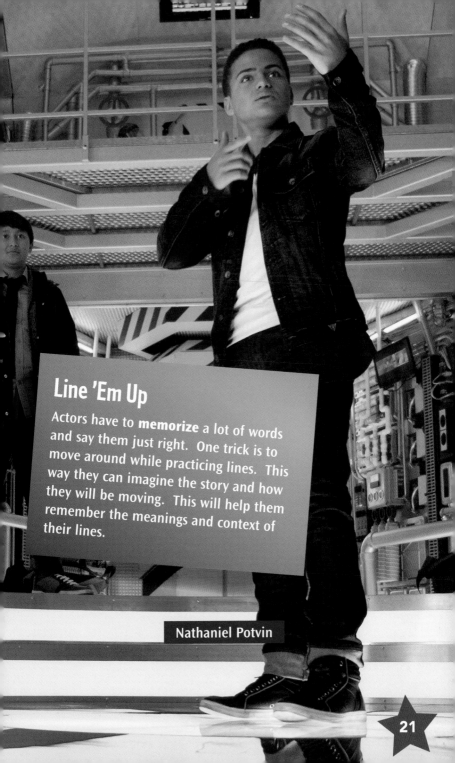

Line 'Em Up

Actors have to **memorize** a lot of words and say them just right. One trick is to move around while practicing lines. This way they can imagine the story and how they will be moving. This will help them remember the meanings and context of their lines.

Nathaniel Potvin

Write Away

Writing is another form of art. People write books, plays, poetry, and more to tell stories and share feelings. No one can give a kid's perspective on life as well as a kid can!

One of the most famous books written by a child is Anne Frank's *The Diary of a Young Girl*. Anne lived in Amsterdam in the Netherlands. She and her family were in hiding during World War II. She kept a diary of her experiences during this terrible time. Tragically, she did not survive the war. But her diary was found, and her father had it published. It has since been published in more than 60 languages.

Poetry All Over

Many poetry competitions are held every year. And kids can participate in quite a few of them. The Foyle Young Poets of the Year award received over 10,000 poems in 2016!

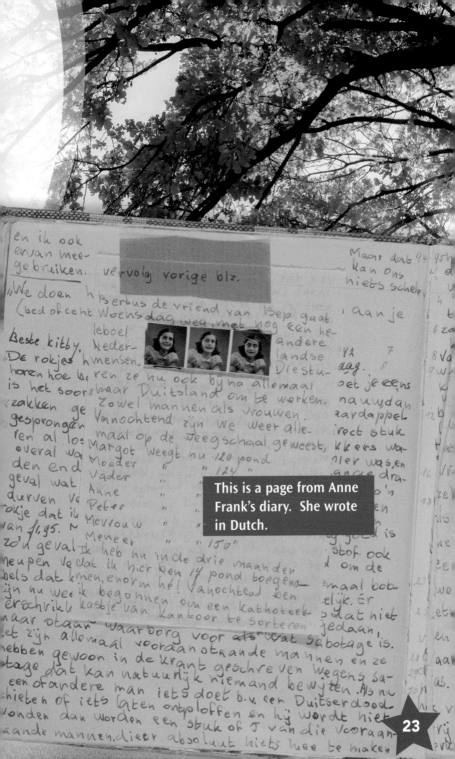

This is a page from Anne Frank's diary. She wrote in Dutch.

Young Authors

Nancy Yi Fan (YEE FAN) was born in China and moved to the United States when she was seven. She wrote her first book, *Swordbird*, when she was 12 years old. She has since written two more books. Nancy's love of birds **inspires** her writing. The main characters in her books are birds.

Some writers use their experiences to create stories. When he was 12, Jake Marcionette (mahr-shuh-NEHT) wrote a book titled *Just Jake* about moving to a new school. Jake was surprised to find that he liked writing. So he decided he would keep writing about his life. Now Just Jake is a popular book series.

Nancy Yi Fan

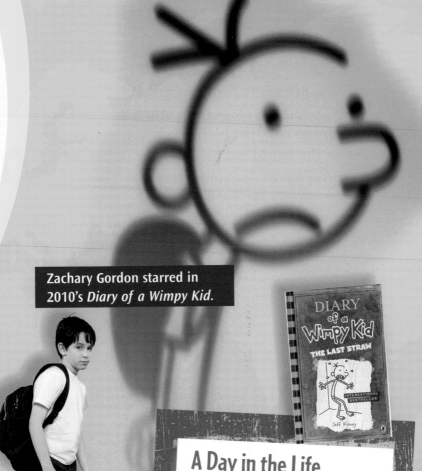

Zachary Gordon starred in 2010's *Diary of a Wimpy Kid*.

DIARY
of a
Wimpy Kid
THE LAST STRAW

INTERNATIONAL BESTSELLER

Jeff Kinney

A Day in the Life

Many authors use moments from their everyday lives in their books. Jeff Kinney writes about his childhood in the Diary of a Wimpy Kid books. Kinney says, "If everyone would write down the funny stories from their own childhoods, the world would be a better place."

Follow Your Art

There are many forms of art and many ways to express yourself. Hopefully, you now realize that nothing can stop people from being creative! Kids all over the world create art every day. Some may even grow up to be famous artists.

Find Your Muse!

In Greek myths, the nine muses were goddesses who inspired humans to create great art. Today, artists call people or things that inspire them their "muses."

Create Something Today!

Now that you have seen so many great ways to create art, try your hand at making something yourself. It doesn't matter how or what. Find a way to express yourself. You can use one of the techniques in this book or find something entirely new!

Float a New Idea or Two

An artist named Christo and his wife, Jeanne-Claude, came up with a new form of art. It was a walkway that floated on a lake. It was made of **buoyant** cubes covered in fabric.

People walk on floating art in Lake Iseo, Italy.

Glossary

abstract—depicting ideas and feelings rather than a specific object or scene

buoyant—able to float

craft—an art that requires special skill

cubism—a style of art in which objects and surfaces are represented by simple shapes

dedicated—having very strong support for a cause

easels—frames for supporting artwork while an artist works on it

express—to make known

inspires—causes something to be created or done

interpret—to bring out the meaning of something

memorize—to commit something to memory

opera—a play where the words are sung and an orchestra plays the music

palettes—thin boards where painters put and mix colors

polio—a disease that attacks the spine and brain and can cause paralysis

solo—alone

watercolors—paints that are mixed with water

Index

Check It Out!

Books

Crilley, Mark. 2016. *The Drawing Lesson: A Graphic Novel That Teaches You How to Draw.* Random House.

Eric Carle Museum. 2007. *Artist to Artist: 23 Major Illustrators Talk to Children About Their Art.*

Reynolds, Peter. 2004. *Ish.* Candlewick Press.

Videos

Andre, Aelita. *Prodigy of Color Exhibition in New York.* www.youtube.com/watch?v =23hWMvSrZx8.

National Gallery of Art. Children's Video Tour: Time Travel. www.nga.gov/education/timetravel /index.shtm.

Websites

Artsonia: World's Largest Student Art Museum. www.artsonia.com.

National Gallery of Art. NGAkids Art Zone. www.nga.gov/content/ngaweb/education /kids.html.

The Poetry Society. Young Poets Network. poetrysociety.org.uk/young-poets/young-poets-network/.

Try It!

Build your own sculptures with papier-mâché. Ask a parent for help before you get started.

- Mix one part flour with one part water in a big bowl. This should give you a thick liquid that looks like glue.

- Next, you'll need an object to use as your basic shape. You can use a balloon.

- Now, take a newspaper, and tear it into long, thin strips (one inch wide).

- Dip the strips in the glue mixture, and place them on your object. Layer them over it until you have newspaper built up all over the object.

- Finally, let it dry overnight. Once it has dried, you have your sculpture! Paint or decorate it as you like.

About the Author

David Paris works with artificial intelligence. This means he helps program computers to think. Recently, David has been using artificial intelligence to help improve video games. He has worked with pirate ships, monsters, people, and robots. He is also very curious and loves to learn about new things!